W9-AUI-777

BRINGING BACK THE

Giant Panda

Ruth Daly

CRABTREE
PUBLISHING COMPANY
WWW.CRABTREEBOOKS.COM

CRABTREE
PUBLISHING COMPANY
WWW.CRABTREEBOOKS.COM

Author: Ruth Daly

Series Research and Development: Reagan Miller

Managing Editor: Tim Cooke

Picture Manager: Sophie Mortimer

Design Manager: Keith Davis

Editorial Director: Lindsey Lowe

Children's Publisher: Anne O'Daly

Editor: Janine Deschenes

Proofreader: Lorna Notsch

Cover design: Margaret Amy Salter

**Production coordinator and
    Prepress technician:** Margaret Amy Salter

Print coordinator: Katherine Berti

Produced for Crabtree Publishing Company
by Brown Bear Books

Photographs (t=top, b= bottom, l=left, r=right, c=center)

Front Cover: All images from Shutterstock

Interior: Alamy: Martyn Evans, 28, Hemis, 6, Minden Pictures, 19t, Xinua, 15t; Avalon: Newscom/Photoshot, 13t, Photoshot/China Photo, 26, Xinhua, 5b, 16, 17b, 18, 27t; Dreamstime: Hans Peter Egert, 27b; Getty Images: Kevin, Zen, 21; GiantPandaGlobal.com: 19b; iStock: Hung Chung Chih, 15b, CraigRJD, 25, Mr B Faust, 10, GoodOlga, 23, guenterguni, 1, 5t, Media Production, 14, Tomas Sereda, 29; Shyam G Menon: Outrigger, 13b; Shutterstock: 12bl, Karel Cerny, 4, Hung chung Chih, 8, Pascale Gueret, 7, Handcraft Films, 12r, Brian Kinney, 24-25, LP2 Studio, 20, moonblack, 11b, SNVV, 11t, World Graphics, 17t.

Brown Bear Books has made every attempt to contact the copyright holder. If you have any information please contact licensing@brownbearbooks.co.uk

Library and Archives Canada Cataloguing in Publication

Daly, Ruth, 1962-, author
        Bringing back the giant panda / Ruth Daly.

(Animals back from the brink)
Includes index.
Issued in print and electronic formats.
ISBN 978-0-7787-4902-8 (hardcover).--
ISBN 978-0-7787-4908-0 (softcover).--
ISBN 978-1-4271-2102-8 (HTML)

        1. Giant panda--Juvenile literature. 2. Giant panda--Conservation--Juvenile literature. 3. Endangered species--Juvenile literature. 4. Wildlife recovery--Juvenile literature. I. Title.

QL737.C27D324 2018   j333.95'978916   C2018-903047-X
                                                                           C2018-903048-8

Library of Congress Cataloging-in-Publication Data

Names: Daly, Ruth, 1962- author.
Title: Bringing back the giant panda / Ruth Daly.
Description: New York, New York : Crabtree Publishing, [2019] |
    Series: Animals back from the brink | Includes index.
Identifiers: LCCN 2018036857 (print) | LCCN 2018037479 (ebook) |
    ISBN 9781427121028 (Electronic) |
    ISBN 9780778749028 (hardcover : alk. paper) |
    ISBN 9780778749080 (paperback : alk. paper)
Subjects: LCSH: Giant panda--Conservation--Juvenile literature.
Classification: LCC QL737.C27 (ebook) |
    LCC QL737.C27 D288 2019 (print) | DDC 599.789--dc23
LC record available at https://lccn.loc.gov/2018036857

Crabtree Publishing Company
www.crabtreebooks.com   1-800-387-7650

Printed in the U.S.A./102018/CG20180810

Published in Canada
Crabtree Publishing
616 Welland Ave.
St. Catharines, Ontario
L2M 5V6

Published in the United States
Crabtree Publishing
PMB 59051
350 Fifth Avenue, 59th Floor
New York, New York 10118

Published in the United Kingdom
Crabtree Publishing
Maritime House
Basin Road North, Hove
BN41 1WR

Published in Australia
Crabtree Publishing
3 Charles Street
Coburg North
VIC, 3058

Contents

Find videos and extra material online at **crabtreeplus.com** to learn more about the conservation of animals and ecosystems. See page 30 in this book for the access code to this material.

The Disappearing Giant Panda

Giant pandas are a type of bear from China. They live only in **coniferous** forests where bamboo grows in the shade of taller trees. They rely on this **habitat** for survival, as they eat mainly bamboo **shoots**, stalks, and roots and make dens, or homes, in hollow tree trunks. However, during the 1900s, the pandas' habitat was destroyed by **logging** to make way for cities, **industry**, and agriculture. As their habitat became smaller, there was less room for pandas to move around and to meet other pandas to have babies with. By 1980, only about 1,000 pandas were thought to survive in the wild. The giant panda became the most **endangered** bear in the world.

Over centuries, giant pandas have been hunted for sport, for use in medicine, and for their pelts, or fur. Chinese superstition, or belief, said that sleeping on panda fur would keep ghosts away.

PANDA FACTS

In their natural habitat, giant pandas now live in China only. In the past, they also lived in Vietnam and Myanmar. Giant pandas can live up to 20 years in the wild, where they travel about 4 miles (6.4 km) per day through their habitat in search of food. They grow between 4 and 5 feet (1.2–1.5 m) tall, and can weigh up to 350 pounds (158 kg). Each giant panda lives alone in its own territory, which it indicates by making marks on trees. Male pandas are called boars. They come together with females, called sows, to **breed**. A sow usually gives birth to a single baby, called a cub, about once every two to three years. Cubs leave their mothers to find their own territory after about 18 months. Like other bears, giant pandas can climb trees.

Giant pandas have a special meaning for the Chinese. Giant pandas are said to have lived in the gardens of the emperors, or Chinese leaders, more than 2,000 years ago. Called da xiong mao in Chinese, the giant panda is today seen as a symbol of peace in China.

Species at Risk

Created in 1984, the International Union for the **Conservation** of Nature (IUCN) protects wildlife, plants, and **natural resources** around the world. Its members include about 1,400 governments and nongovernmental organizations. The IUCN publishes the Red List of Threatened **Species** each year, which tells people how likely a plant or animal species is to become **extinct**. It began publishing the list in 1964.

SCIENTIFIC CRITERIA

The Red List, created by scientists, divides nearly 80,000 species of plants and animals into nine categories. Criteria for each category include the growth and **decline** of the population size of a species. They also include how many individuals within a species can breed, or have babies. In addition, scientists include information about the habitat of the species, such as its size and quality. These criteria allow scientists to figure out the probability of extinction facing the species.

The Pyrenean ibex that lived in the mountains between France and Spain was last recorded by the IUCN in 2000. It is now classed as **Extinct** (EX). The IUCN updates the Red List twice a year to track the changing of species. Each individual species is reevaluated at least every five years.

IUCN LEVELS OF THREAT

The Red List uses nine categories to define the threat to a species.

Extinct (EX)	No living individuals survive
Extinct in the Wild (EW)	Species cannot be found in its natural habitat. Exists only in **captivity**, in **cultivation**, or in an area that is not its natural habitat.
Critically Endangered (CR)	At extremely high risk of becoming extinct in the wild
Endangered (EN)	At very high risk of extinction in the wild
Vulnerable (VU)	At high risk of extinction in the wild
Near Threatened (NT)	Likely to become threatened in the near future
Least Concern (LC)	Widespread, abundant, or at low risk
Data Deficient (DD)	Not enough data to make a judgment about the species
Not Evaluated (NE)	Not yet evaluated against the criteria

In the United States, the Endangered Species Act of 1973 was passed to protect species from possible extinction. It has its own criteria for classifying species, but they are similar to those of the IUCN. Canada introduced the Species at Risk Act in 2002. More than 530 species are protected under the act. The list of species is compiled by the Committee on the Status of Endangered Wildlife in Canada (COSEWIC).

GIANT PANDAS AT RISK

The IUCN Red List classified the giant panda as Endangered (EN) in 1990. It had previously classified the panda as Rare, a classification that is no longer used. In 2016, the Red List upgraded the giant panda's status to Vulnerable (VU), following a 17 percent rise in the population over the previous decade.

Losing the Panda Habitat

In the 1940s, the Chinese government realized that hunting and habitat destruction were causing a large reduction in the number of giant pandas. It passed laws to try to protect the bears. Each **province** had to provide land where wildlife, such as giant pandas, could live in their natural habitats. However, the government's efforts did not work. Despite setting aside land for wildlife, about 30 percent of the forests in China were destroyed in the 50 years that followed. Many trees were cut down to make room for a growing Chinese population and for industries such as ironmaking. The giant panda population continued to fall. Between 1975 and 1984, its habitat shrank from about 11,500 square miles (30,000 sq km) to approximately 5,000 square miles (13,000 sq km).

As large areas of bamboo forest were cleared beginning in the 1940s, the giant pandas moved higher up mountain slopes. Their once-large habitat was broken up by cities and roads into smaller sections. This separated panda communities.

COLLABORATING FOR A CAUSE

As the panda habitat was shrinking, people began taking measures to protect the giant panda. In the 1960s, Sichuan Province in China created special **reserves** to protect wildlife, including giant pandas. Later, in 1981, China joined the Convention on the International Trade in Endangered Species (CITES). This made it illegal to trade panda pelts, which lowered the number of pandas that were killed by hunters. In 1988, the Wildlife Protection Act gave giant pandas protected status in China. This made it illegal to hunt giant pandas. Anyone caught **poaching** faced strict penalties, including life imprisonment.

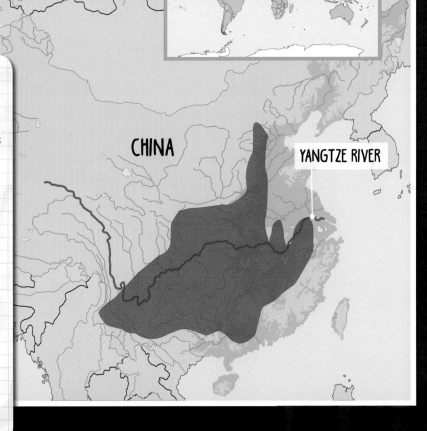

GIANT PANDA, HISTORICAL RANGE

CHINA

CHINA

YANGTZE RIVER

The panda's traditional **range** lay in the Yangtze River **Basin**, which is one of the most heavily populated parts of China today. As the population grew and humans settled there, the range slowly shrank. The rise of industry shrank this range, too. This region produces half of China's grain and 70 percent of its rice and fish. It is home to mines, industries, cities, and farmland.

Key

Activity ranges

■ Historic range (up to 18th century)

0   500 miles

800 km

Giant Pandas in the Ecosystem

The giant panda is an **umbrella species** in the bamboo forest **ecosystem**. This means that when a giant panda's needs are met within its ecosystem, its likely that the needs of the other species that live in that ecosystem also are being met. Giant pandas are important parts of their ecosystem. They are mainly herbivores. Their **diet** consists almost entirely of bamboo, although they also eat fish, flowers, and small mammals. As they roam, giant pandas spread bamboo seeds through their waste, helping vegetation to spread to new areas. With lower panda populations, the plant life in a bamboo forest ecosystem cannot flourish, because the seeds cannot be spread. Since other animals, such as the lemur, also rely on bamboo to survive, their populations may decline, too, along with the panda's.

Bamboo is a poor food. Most parts of the plant are low in protein. This means that giant pandas have to eat a lot of it to stay healthy. A giant panda eats between 20 and 80 pounds (10-35 kg) of bamboo every day!

A MENU OF BAMBOO

More than 400 types of bamboo grow in China, of which giant pandas feed on about 40. Giant pandas spend about 12 hours every day eating. Bamboo is a tough plant, which makes it hard to chew and digest, or break down in the stomach. Giant pandas have strong linings in their throat and stomach to help digest bamboo. However, bamboo only flowers once every 20 to 120 years, and then it dies. In the past, giant pandas simply moved to find new sources of bamboo. But today, it is impossible for them to move because there are cities and roads blocking their way.

Some species in the bamboo forest are **endemic**, which means they are only found in the bamboo forest ecosystem. Endemic species such as the golden pheasant only live in the bamboo forest and heavily depend on it. If one species, such as the giant panda, is lost from the habitat, it could result in the loss of others, too.

Who Got Involved?

In the 1970s, the government of China began to hold surveys every 10 years to **monitor** giant pandas in the wild. The government also made panda habitats safer by arresting poachers and stopping human activities in these areas. Whole towns were moved to new locations outside of the giant pandas' habitats. International organizations also became involved in giant panda conservation efforts, including the World Wildlife Fund (WWF). The WWF was originally founded in 1961 to help protect endangered species around the world. In 1980, it became the first international conservation organization to work in China. Some of its work includes increasing giant panda habitats and creating **green corridors** that join habitats together.

Since the 1980s, all giant pandas have been owned by the government of China. The Chinese government loans giant pandas to zoos around the world, but even panda cubs born in zoos in other countries belong to China.

The WWF logo is an image of a giant panda.

WWF

COLLABORATING FOR A CAUSE

A range of organizations joined the struggle to save the giant panda. Pandas International was founded in 2000 by Suzanne Braden and Diane Reese. Its main purposes are to raise awareness by providing information about the challenges faced by giant pandas and to raise money to help panda centers in China. Panda reserves breed pandas in **captivity**, help restore their habitat, and care for sick and injured pandas. The centers are also involved with researching panda behavior, nutrition, and breeding. Money raised by Pandas International provides supplies to panda centers, such as milk formula to feed panda cubs (right), and equipment for playing, such as swings.

Collaboration has been an important part of the panda conservation effort. In 1980, Dr. George Schaller of the WWF was invited to work with the Chinese government and scientists studying giant pandas.

Save the Forests!

Saving bamboo forests has been an important part of the fight to save giant pandas. Not only do the forests provide their habitat, but bamboo is also their main source of food. The Chinese government banned logging in forests where giant pandas were known to live. It also created programs that pay farmers money if they replace crops with forests, or plant trees instead of using land for logging. Farmers also receive money for not using chemicals to kill pests or feed their crops, since these harm the environment. Another step to benefit pandas was to reduce **erosion**. With fewer trees, much more land in the bamboo forest was eroded, or washed away, when the Yangtze River flooded. Past floods have destroyed animal habitats, including those of the giant panda. The Grain to Green program set up by the Chinese government encourages farmers to plant trees. Trees help to slow the process of erosion and help reduce the impact of floods when they happen.

One key part of protecting the giant panda has been educating communities who share the animals' habitat. The WWF and Pandas International have worked with local communities to help them establish ways of farming that will not have negative impacts on the panda population.

Visitors can learn about conservation and the benefits of tourism at panda reserves. The reserves provide information through displays and exhibits. Many have panda cams set up in the forest, which allow visitors to watch pandas in their natural habitat.

COLLABORATING FOR A CAUSE

The Chinese government set up the first panda reserve in 1963 in southern China to provide a safe place for pandas to live. Since then, other organizations, including the WWF, have established more reserves. Today, 67 reserves protect approximately 346,000 acres (1.4 million hectares) of giant panda habitat. These reserves are home to 70 percent of wild giant pandas. Regular patrols monitor the reserves for poaching and check the health of giant pandas. Some reserves have panda hospitals and research laboratories, and many provide education for tourists about reducing the human impact on giant pandas. By watching panda cams set up in the reserves, visitors and even people at home can see giant pandas going about their daily routines and interacting with each other (right).

Conservation in Action

One serious problem faced by giant pandas is that their habitat is **fragmented**. This means that the once-large habitat where pandas used to roam freely is now separated into different, smaller habitats. Giant pandas need to move between habitats to find more bamboo when it dies off in one place. They also need to move to find mates, or other giant pandas they can have babies with. This increases the giant panda population. China's State Forestry Administration is working to create green corridors, natural pathways that connect separate habitats with each other. Wildlife can use them to travel safely from one habitat to another. The corridors are planted with the same types of vegetation, or plants, that are found in the natural habitats.

Panda centers provide bases for scientific research into panda behavior. They also oversee captive breeding programs, in which cubs are raised at the center and prepared for their eventual release into the wild.

CREATING CORRIDORS

For the giant panda, green corridors are planted with bamboo, along with other **native** plant species. Bamboo grows quickly, which means the corridors can be ready for pandas to use only a few years after they have been planted. In a green corridor, there are no roads or railroads, no hiking trails or towns—no human activity at all. This provides a safe way for pandas to move to other areas when they need to find a new source of bamboo or to find a mate.

A bamboo **reforestation** project at the Wolong Panda Center discovered the five types of bamboo that giant pandas seem to prefer. By planting these species in the green corridors, pandas are encouraged to use them.

The Wolong Panda Center is part of the Wolong National Nature Reserve in Sichuan Province. It was set up by the WWF and the Chinese government in 1980. By 2018, scientists at the center had successfully bred 66 healthy giant panda cubs.

An International Panda Plan

To help increase the giant panda population, China has set up an international breeding plan, which has placed giant pandas at zoos all around the world. Zoos lease, or borrow, pandas from the Chinese government for $1 million per year and return the animals after the agreed time period, usually after five or 10 years. The zoos also have to pay China for any cubs born during the pandas' stay. The money paid to China is used for the preservation of pandas still living in the wild there. Zoos around the world help raise awareness about giant pandas, and carry out research and breeding programs. There are usually about a dozen giant pandas in the United States at zoos in Washington, D.C., San Diego, Atlanta, and Memphis. In Canada, a giant panda family lives at Calgary Zoo.

Baby giant pandas are very fragile. They are born blind and without hair, which begins to grow after two or three weeks. The cubs also begin to crawl at about the same time, but they cannot walk until they are three months old. Since they are so weak, breeding baby giant pandas successfully can be extremely difficult.

In 2008, an earthquake devastated the Wolong Panda Center (left). Of the 63 giant pandas then at the center, two died, and large areas of the national reserve were destroyed. Several wild pandas came down from the mountains searching for food, but it is not known how many wild pandas were killed.

LEADING THE RESEARCH EFFORT

Today, panda centers and reserves in China lead the way in research into giant pandas. The Dijiangyan Giant Panda Base, for example, has a hospital and a laboratory. It treats wild pandas that are sick and injured (below right). The base also cares for older pandas or those that have been disabled in some way. Research laboratories at panda centers help to prevent the spread of disease. Scientists study the diseases that affect pandas and look for ways to control and treat them. Giant pandas can suffer from a variety of health problems, including digestive diseases, becoming overheated in the sun, and illnesses that affect their breathing.

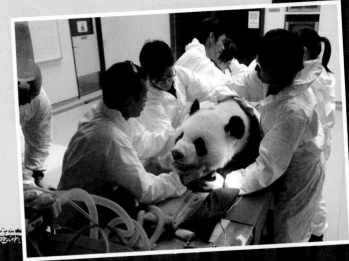

Back from the Brink!

Today, giant pandas can only be found living in the wild in the Chinese provinces of Sichuan, Shaanxiu, and Gansu, located in southwestern China. By establishing 67 giant panda reserves, the government of China has begun to increase the areas of bamboo forest within the giant panda habitat. This has encouraged population growth among the pandas. A new project, announced in 2018, plans to link the 67 panda reserves together to create one huge reserve. It will be approximately 10,475 square miles (27,135 sq km) in area, covering parts of all three provinces where giant pandas still remain. The project is expected to cost about $1.5 billion.

Restoring and preserving their habitat, plus a ban on hunting, has led to an increase in the giant panda population. By 2004, there were 1,596 giant pandas living in the wild, and by 2014, this number had risen to 1,864. On September 4, 2016, the IUCN upgraded the pandas' status from Endangered to Vulnerable.

PROTECTION FROM POACHERS

Making hunting illegal helped to reduce the decline in the panda population. Poaching remains a threat to the pandas, but it is not as widespread as in the past. One of the biggest risks to pandas in the wild is from hunters who are targeting other animals, such as deer. Giant pandas are sometimes injured or killed when they become accidentally caught in traps meant for these other animals.

GIANT PANDA RANGE, 2018

CHINA

Today, giant pandas are limited to fragmented regions in mountainous southwestern China. This region is also home to millions of people, which puts pressure on the pandas' natural habitat. The range of the giant panda may increase when the Chinese government completes its plan to connect all of the individual panda reserves with green corridors.

CHINA

YANGTZE RIVER

Key

■ 2018 range

0   500 miles
|————————|
     800 km

Panda Cubs around the World

Jia Panpan and his sister, Jia Yueyue, were born at the Toronto Zoo in 2015. They were the first giant panda cubs to be born in Canada. In 2012, Canada joined the international giant panda breeding program with China and agreed to host two pandas for 10 years, beginning in 2013. In 2018, the cubs and their parents moved to the zoo in Calgary to spend the second half of their time in Canada. The United States joined the panda breeding program when it began in the 1980s. As part of the program, a cub named Bei Bei was born at the National Zoo in Washington, D.C., in 2015. The cub is expected to move to China at the age of four.

Calgary Zoo provides 88 pounds (40 kg) of fresh bamboo for Jia Panpan and Jia Yueyue every day. Bamboo does not grow in Canada, so it is flown in from the mountains of Sichuan Province in China. It is one reason hosting the pandas is expensive! Zoos also have to build special enclosures and pay leasing fees.

HEADING HOME

Visitors to giant panda reserves in China might see pandas that were born all over the world. No matter where they are born, all giant panda cubs must be returned to China at the age of about four. This enables the Chinese government to monitor the global panda population and develop the international breeding program. Although it might seem cruel to separate young pandas from their parents, in fact, it follows what happens in the wild. Because giant pandas live alone in their own territory, panda cubs usually leave their mothers before the age of two in order to find and establish a territory of their own.

Despite the progress that has been made in bringing giant pandas back from the brink, some people believe the animals are not worth the huge cost of saving them from extinction. Many Chinese people are poor, yet the government spends large amounts of money on bamboo restoration and maintenance, giant panda breeding programs, and research projects.

Saving Other Species

Because the giant panda is an umbrella species, the efforts to protect it have also resulted in benefits to other threatened species in the bamboo forest ecosystem. About 70 percent of China's forest birds and mammals live in the habitat. The mammals include the takin, which is classed as Vulnerable. Protecting and enlarging the forests will give species such as these more food sources and larger territories. The lessons learned over years of international cooperation to save the giant panda can also be applied to save threatened animals in other ecosystems on Earth. One lesson is that it takes a long time to restore forests. It took decades to replant bamboo forests and establish green corridors that have helped improve the giant panda habitat. Another important lesson is the importance of building reserves and centers that focus on species protection and research. The importance of international cooperation also has been learned. Many organizations around the world work together to save the giant panda.

ANOTHER ENDANGERED BEAR

The koala (below) is a mammal endemic to Australia. Just as the giant panda depends on bamboo for its habitat and food, koalas depend on eucalyptus trees. Both the koala and giant panda are beloved animals around the world and are each considered to be icons of their countries. The two animals also share some other similarities. The koala population is declining for some of the same reasons as those affecting giant pandas. Koalas were hunted in the past, and they now face challenges from the loss and fragmentation of their habitat. This is due to human development and rising global temperatures. Other threats include disease, malnutrition, and being killed or injured in traffic accidents or attacks from pets, such as dogs. The IUCN listed koalas as Vulnerable in 2016. It is possible that some of the lessons learned from the great panda conservation efforts, such as creating green corridors, could be applied to help increase the koala population.

In 2015, researchers found that there are some threatened endemic species that are not helped by panda conservation efforts, because their habitats are mostly outside of where the panda lives. The golden snub-nosed monkey (left) is one of these species. The researchers recommended ways that the Chinese government can protect these species, too.

Looking to the Future

The giant panda population is increasing. Giant panda cubs born in captivity have been released into the wild in China as part of conservation programs. Despite the successful work to preserve bamboo habitats, however, a serious threat to giant pandas and their habitat remains. This threat is **climate change**. Global temperatures are rising. Scientists are studying the impact of this change in temperature on bamboo. They predict that up to one-third of the giant pandas' habitat could be destroyed in the next 80 years if the climate becomes too warm for bamboo to grow. This could result in a decline in the giant pandas that depend on bamboo for their food.

Giant pandas that have been born in captivity are usually reintroduced in areas that are already home to small populations of pandas. Their eating habits, movements, and behavior are closely monitored.

TOURISM

Tourists hoping to see a giant panda in its natural habitat sometimes venture into the bamboo forests where the pandas live. Although tourism brings money to the local region, any kind of human activity in giant panda habitats disturbs the ecosystem. Since the habitat is already at risk, all tourism needs to be managed carefully so that it does not negatively impact the animals. The Chinese government encourages tourists who want to see giant pandas to visit giant panda centers instead (right).

KEEPING PANDAS HEALTHY

Wherever bamboo grows, bamboo rats (below) can be also be found. These rodents can pass on diseases that easily spread through the giant panda community. Some diseases can cause giant pandas in the wild to become so weak, they will die without medical treatment. **Parasites** are another problem. One type of worm that lives only in giant pandas causes an infection that damages the stomach and can eventually affect the eyes and brain. It is difficult to prevent this infection because it is spread through panda waste, of which there is always a large amount. There is no cure, but it can be treated with medication. However, as there is no cure, it poses a serious threat to the future of giant pandas that live in the wild.

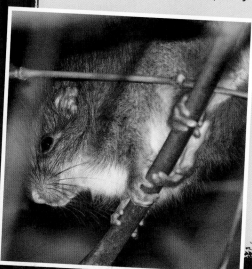

The Giant Panda Needs You!

Around the world, many goods are made from bamboo. It is popular because it grows quickly. Bamboo is used to make all sorts of things, ranging from mats and furniture to chopsticks, musical instruments, and paper. In China, it is also used in some traditional medicines. But giant pandas are directly harmed when bamboo forests are logged. Saving paper, and avoiding products that are made from bamboo, are some ways that people can help to protect the giant panda.

In 2015, China used bamboo to produce about 9 million tons (8.1 million metric tonnes) of household paper, such as napkins, tissues, toilet paper, and paper towels. Choosing reusable products or products made from recycled paper can help reduce paper consumption.

Since the last decades of the 1900s, China has built many factories. These factories release smoke and harmful gases into the air. Some people are concerned that China's factories do not do enough to limit pollution.

REDUCING GREENHOUSE GASES

One of the most serious threats facing the bamboo forests and giant pandas is climate change. One cause of climate change is the release of greenhouse gases from industry and some transportation into the air. These cause global temperatures to rise. You can take action to reduce climate change and help giant pandas by following the tips below.

- Write your elected representatives and make the case for taking measures to reduce greenhouse gases and prevent climate change.

- Make ecological choices when you travel. One way to reduce greenhouse gas emissions is to carpool. When more people travel in the same vehicle, fewer cars are used, and fewer greenhouse gases are released into the atmosphere.

- If you have to fly, use airlines that have high occupancy rates, which means the airplanes carry more travelers. This helps reduce greenhouse gases, because fewer airplanes will be used to transport people from one place to another.

Learning More

Books

Bodden, Valerie. *Amazing Animals: Pandas.* Creative Education, 2013.

Haugen, Brenda. *Giant Pandas. Endangered and Threatened Animals.* Capstone Press, 2012.

Jazynka, Kitson. *Mission: Panda Rescue: All About Pandas and How to Save Them.* National Geographic Kids, 2016.

Katirgis, Jane. *Endangered Giant Pandas. Wildlife at Risk.* Enslow Publishing Inc, 2015.

Thimmesh, Catherine. *Camp Panda: Training Cubs to Survive in the Wild.* Houghton Mifflin Harcourt, 2018.

On the Web

www.bearsoftheworld.net/giant_panda_bears.asp
This site compares giant pandas with other members of the bear family using pictures and basic facts.

www.giantpandaglobal.com
This site provides information about giant pandas living at zoos and breeding centers around the world.

www.nationalgeographic.org/game/panda-wild
This National Geographic page allows readers to design their own reserves to meet a giant panda's needs.

www.pandasinternational.org
The Pandas International site describes the work of the organization and contains information about giant pandas, including videos, photographs, and cool facts.

www.zooatlanta.org/animal/giant-panda
The Atlanta Zoo has a live panda cam that lets you watch pandas in real time, plus other facts and photographs.

For videos, activities, and more, enter the access code at the Crabtree Plus website below.

www.crabtreeplus.com/animals-back-brink

Access code: abb37

Glossary

basin The area drained by a river

breed To mate and produce offspring

captivity A situation in which an animal is held in a zoo or conservation center and taken care of by humans

climate change A change in normal global weather patterns thought to be caused in part by human activity

coniferous Made up of evergreen trees and shrubs that do not lose their leaves in winter

conservation The preserving and protecting of plants, animals, and natural resources

cultivation The artificial breeding and planting of plants, such as crops

decline To fall in number

diet The range of food eaten by a type of animal

ecosystem Everything that exists in a particular environment, including animals and plants and nonliving things, such as soil and sunlight

endangered In danger of becoming extinct

endemic Describing a species that is only found in a specific location

erosion The process of being worn away by wind or water

extinct Describes a situation in which all members of a species have died, so the species no longer exists

fragmented Separated or broken up

green corridors Strips of land with vegetation that allow animals to pass easily along them

habitat The natural surroundings in which an animal lives

industry Processing raw materials and manufacturing goods in factories

logging Cutting down trees for their wood

monitor To observe something closely and record information

native Naturally occurring in a particular place

natural resources Useful materials that occur in nature

parasites Organisms that live on or inside living things, usually harming their hosts

poaching The illegal hunting and killing of animals

province A region of China with its own local government

range The region where an animal lives, or the distance it regularly moves

reforestation The large-scale planting of trees to replace those that have been cut down

reserves Protected places where animals can live safely

shoots Young branches or leaves of a tree or plant

species A group of similar animals or plants that can breed with one another

umbrella species A species whose health is a sign of the health of a whole ecosystem

Index and About the Author

ABOUT THE AUTHOR

Ruth Daly has more than 25 years teaching experience, mainly in elementary schools, and she currently teaches Grade 3. She has written more than 30 nonfiction books for the education market on a wide range of subjects and for a variety of age groups. These include books on animals, life cycles, and the natural environment. Her fiction and poetry have been published in magazines and literary journals.